Sports Are the Best!

FOOTBALL IS THE BEST!

by Joe Tischler

PEBBLE
a capstone imprint

Pebble is published by Capstone,
1710 Roe Crest Drive, North Mankato, Minnesota 56003
capstonepub.com

Library of Congress Cataloging-in-Publication Data is available on the Library of Congress website.

ISBN: 9798875256233 (hardcover)
ISBN: 9798875256189 (paperback)
ISBN: 9798875256196 (ebook pdf)

Summary: Easy-to-read text and bright photographs describe the rules, positions, skills, stars, and more of football. A short quiz at the end of the book lets the reader test what they've learned.

Editorial Credits
Editor: Erika L. Shores; Designer: Hilary Wacholz; Media Researcher: Rebekah Hubstenberger; Production Specialist: Tori Abraham

Image Credits
Associated Press: AJ Mast, 5; Getty Images: Brian Bahr, 18, Cavan Images, 26, Cavan Images/Lisa Weatherbee, 27, Chris Coduto, 20, Dustin Bradford, 23, Dylan Buell, 19, Ezra Shaw, 9, Fuse, cover (right), iStock/cmannphoto, 15, iStock/Joseph Calomeni, cover (left), Jared C. Tilton, 21, Joe Sargent, 11, Kevin Dodge, 12, Michael Hickey, 7, Nic Antaya, 17, Norm Hall, 24, Ronald Martinez, 6, Timothy T Ludwig, 25, Todd Olszewski, 8; Shutterstock: grey_and (football), back cover, spine, and throughout, halwani wani (net), throughout, JoeSAPhotos, cover (middle), Lopolo, 29, Mtsaride, 13, shocky, 14

Printed and bound in China. 006459

Table of Contents

Touchdown! 4

A Team Sport 10

Football Rules 14

Football Positions 18

Football Skills 24

Is Football the Best? 28

Test Your Football Knowledge 30
Glossary 31
Index 32
About the Author 32

Words in **bold** are in the glossary.

Touchdown!

A **quarterback** throws the ball down the field. The crowd cheers. Your favorite team just scored. You are at a football game!

Football is the most popular sport in the United States. The **NFL Super Bowl** is the most watched TV event every year. What is it that makes football so popular?

RECEIVING
TARGETS
RECEPTIONS
YARDS
YARDS AFTER CATCH
VISA
CHIEFS
NFL
EAGLES

Football is fun to watch. Going to a game in person is a thrill. You can celebrate with fans near you. Some college stadiums hold more than 100,000 people. You can also watch at home on TV. Replays of great catches are exciting.

High school football games are played on Friday nights. College football is played on Saturdays. NFL games are on Sundays, Mondays, and Thursdays.

Justin Jefferson

Football fans cheer for star players. Justin Jefferson makes awesome catches. J.J. Watt plays **defense**. He makes a lot of quarterback **sacks.**

Quarterback Patrick Mahomes has won two NFL Most Valuable Player (MVP) awards. He also has won three Super Bowls for the Kansas City Chiefs.

Patrick Mahomes

A Team Sport

Football is fun because it's a team sport. It takes more than one great player to win a game. A quarterback needs **blocking** from players on **offense**. The receivers need to be good at handling the ball. Defensive players work together to stop the other team from scoring.

Running back Najee Harris (in black) faces off against the Dallas Cowboys defense.

What equipment does a football team need? Pads and helmets protect players' bodies. Shoes called cleats help grip the ground. Players wear jerseys, pants, and long socks. Jerseys often have the player's last name and number on the back.

You can't play football without a ball. A football is made of leather. It has laces on one side. Quarterbacks use the laces to help throw **spirals**.

Football Rules

Football is played on a 100-yard field. At each end is a 10-yard end zone. The offense works to get the ball into the other team's end zone. The defense tries to stop them. A touchdown is when a team gets the ball into the end zone. It is six points.

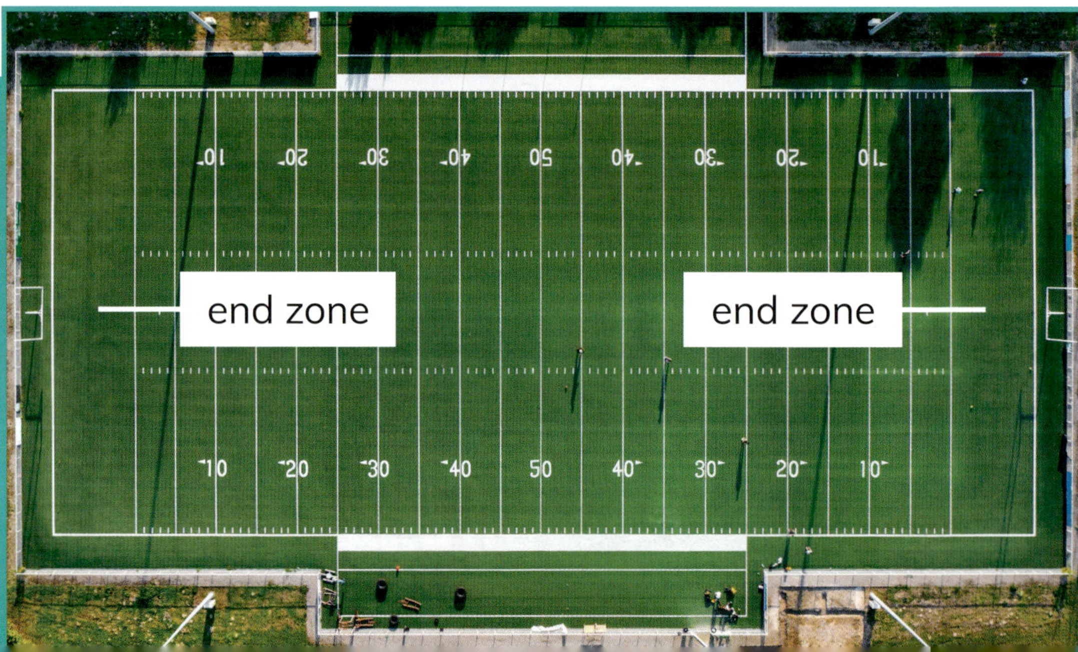

Teams can score without getting a touchdown. At the back of the end zone are goalposts. An offense can try to kick the ball between the posts. A made field goal is three points.

An offense moves down the field to score. They must get first downs along the way. A first down is 10 yards long.

An offense has four tries to gain 10 yards. If they get 10 yards, they keep moving down the field. If they don't get 10 yards, the ball goes to the other team's offense. A play ends when the runner is tackled or goes out of bounds.

Football Positions

During a game, 11 offensive and 11 defensive players are on the field. The quarterback leads the offense. They call out the plays. The quarterback can throw a pass. Other plays involve giving a running back the ball or running with it themselves.

In front of the quarterback is the offensive line. They work to stop the other team by blocking.

The defense has three stages of defenders. The first is the defensive line. It usually has two defensive tackles and two ends. These players try to tackle the quarterback.

The next stage are the linebackers. They try to tackle the running back. The cornerbacks and safeties are the last stage. They guard the wide receivers.

Linebacker Shaq Thompson (in white) tackles running back James Conner (in red).

The special teams take the field when a team kicks the ball. A kicker tries to make field goals and extra points. A punter kicks the ball to the other team.

What happens if the offense has not gained 10 yards on three plays? The special teams either punts, or the offense tries for the first down.

SMITH

Football Skills

In football, a player has many ways to help their team. Speed and **endurance** are important. Wide receivers, cornerbacks, and safeties are the fastest players on the field. They run the most.

Wide receiver Ja'Marr Chase (in white) runs with the ball.

Quarterback Josh Allen throws a pass.

Quarterbacks need to be accurate with their passes. They need to see who is open down the field while facing the defense.

What do all football players need? Mental toughness! It helps them keep trying and never give up.

What can a player do to help their team win? They work on throwing and catching. They practice blocking and tackling. Running and kicking are other great football skills to improve.

Is Football the Best?

Football is played in different seasons. Teams hold training camps in summer. Regular season games happen in fall. **Playoff** games take place in winter. No matter the weather, you can enjoy playing and watching football with family and friends.

What do you like best about football?

Test Your Football Knowledge

Now that you've read this book, are you a football expert? Take this quiz to find out! If you don't know the answer, read the book again and you might be able to find it.

1. What group of players handles kicking the ball for extra points?

    a. Linebackers

    b. Cornerbacks

    c. Special teams

2. How many defensive players are on the field at a time?

    a. 7

    b. 11

    c. 13

3. What position is called the leader of the offense?

    a. Quarterback

    b. Punter

    c. Wide receiver

Answers: 1c, 2b, 3a

Glossary

blocking (BLOK-ing)—movements where one player uses their body to stop another player's path forward

defense (di-FENS)—the team that does not have possession of the ball; this team tries to keep the offensive team from getting the ball into their end zone

endurance (en-DUR-enss)—the act of doing something for longer periods of time

NFL Super Bowl (en-f-EL SOO-pur BOL)—the championship game of the National Football League (NFL)

offense (aw-FENSS)—the team in control of the ball and trying to score

playoff (PLAY-awf)—a series of games played after the regular season to decide a championship

quarterback (KWOR-tur-bak)—the player who runs the offense; the quarterback can run, hand off the ball, or make a pass

sack (SAK)—a play where the quarterback is tackled behind the line of scrimmage

spiral (SPY-ruhl)—a throw that spins the ball along an imaginary straight line

Index

blocking, 10, 19, 27
defense, 8, 10, 14, 18, 20, 25
endurance, 24
equipment, 12
field goals, 15, 22
first downs, 16, 22
Jefferson, Justin, 8
Mahomes, Patrick, 9
NFL Super Bowl, 4, 9
offense, 10, 14, 15, 16, 18, 19, 22
quarterbacks, 4, 8, 9, 10, 13, 18, 19, 20, 25
running, 18, 24, 27
sacking, 8
special teams, 22
tackling, 16, 20, 21, 27
throwing, 4, 13, 18, 25, 27
touchdowns, 14, 15
Watt, J.J., 8

About the Author

Joe Tischler is an author and sportswriter who lives in southern Minnesota. When he's not writing about sports, he's watching sports. As a lifelong Minnesotan, he is an avid fan of Minnesota sports teams including the Vikings, Twins, Timberwolves, and Golden Gophers. He's happily married to Gwen and is a proud father to son Toby.